THE BATHROOM SUPER BOWL QUIZ BOOK

by

Jack Kreismer

RED-LETTER PRESS, INC.
Saddle River, New Jersey

THE BATHROOM SUPER BOWL QUIZ BOOK
Copyright ©2003 Red-Letter Press, Inc.
ISBN: 0-940462-36-2
All Rights Reserved
Printed in the United States of America

For information address:

Red-Letter Press, Inc.
P.O. Box 393, Saddle River, NJ 07458
www.Red-LetterPress.com

ACKNOWLEDGMENTS

Project Development Coordinator:
Kobus Reyneke

Cover design and typography:
s.w.artz, inc.

Editorial:
Jeff Kreismer

Significant Others:
Theresa Adragna
Kathy Hoyt, Robin Kreismer
Jim & Rory Tomlinson, Lori Walsh

INTRODUCTION

For more than twenty years, the original Bathroom Library has entertained people on the go everywhere. With millions of copies out there, it proves that we're not all wet about bathroom reading.

Now, as heir to the throne, we proudly introduce a brand new Bathroom Library. We hope you enjoy this installment of it.

Yours flushingly,

Jack Kreismer
Publisher

FOR AMERICA'S
FAVORITE READING ROOM

THE
BATHROOM
SUPER BOWL
QUIZ BOOK

*A Royal Flush of
Pigskin Puzzlers*

THE BATHROOM LIBRARY

RED-LETTER PRESS, INC.
Saddle River, New Jersey

FIRST AND TEN

1. How much did tickets cost for the "cheap seats" in the first Super Bowl?

2. What network televised Super Bowl I?

3. Who played in the first Super Bowl and, for extra credit, what was the score?

4. Where was it played?

5. He caught only four passes during the regular season yet grabbed eight in the first Super Bowl. Name him.

6. Who was the first man to play in a Super Bowl and later take a team to the big game as a head coach?

7. What was the first wild card team to win a Super Bowl?

8. Do you know the team which became the first to win three Super Bowls in a four season span? Hint: think '90s.

9. Who was the first player in Super Bowl history to return a kickoff for a touchdown while playing on the winning team?

10. Who was the first Super Bowl player to become a member of *Monday Night Football's* broadcast team?

EXTRA POINT

"The NFL, like life, is full of idiots."

-*Randy Cross,* 49ers Super Bowl offensive lineman

ANSWERS

1. $6 (Choice seats were $12.)

2. Both CBS and NBC.

3. Green Bay defeated Kansas City, 35-10.

4. The Los Angeles Coliseum.

5. Max McGee.

6. Forrest Gregg ... He played for the Packers in Super Bowls I and II and coached the Bengals in Super Bowl XVI.

7. The Oakland Raiders, 27-10 over Philadelphia, in Super Bowl XV.

8. The Dallas Cowboys.

9. Desmond Howard, for the Packers against the Patriots in Super Bowl XXXI.

10. Fran Tarkenton, in 1979.

EXTRA POINT

"After 12 years, the old butterflies come back.
Well, I guess at my age you can call them moths."

-*Franco Harris*, on playing with the Seahawks
after 12 years and four Super Bowl
championship teams with the Steelers

THE COIN TOSS

*Up until Super Bowl XII, officials handled the pre-game
coin toss. Since then, there have been honorees.
See how many you can identify from the clues provided.*

1. The Galloping Ghost handled the coin toss before the
Broncos-Cowboys game in 1978.

2. In 1979, before the Cowboys-Steelers game, the coin flip was
made by a man who played right field for the Yankees before
Babe Ruth.

3. Crazy Legs was accorded the honors before Super Bowl XVII
between the Redskins and Dolphins.

4. Flipping the coin before the Raiders-Redskins contest in 1984
was a Bears fullback in the 1930s who was a charter member
of the Pro Football Hall of Fame.

5. When the Giants and Broncos clashed in 1987, this Hall of
Fame Green Bay defensive end in the sixties handled the
pre-game task.

6. This coin flipper, prior to Super Bowl XXII's Redskins-
Broncos clash, was a receiver and defensive back for the
Packers from 1935-'45.

7. The commissioner before Paul Tagliabue flipped the coin at
the Giants-Bills game in 1991.

8. The Dallas-Buffalo Super Bowl XXVIII pre-game coin flip was
made by a quarterback who played in ten consecutive title
games for the Browns in the 1940s and '50s.

9. At the Super Bowl's thirtieth anniversary when the Cowboys
opposed the Steelers in 1996, the coin was tossed by a man
who's won three MVPs in the big game.

10. The coach of the Chiefs only championship team did the
honors before Super Bowl XXXI.

ANSWERS

1. Red Grange.

2. "Papa Bear," George Halas.

3. Elroy Hirsch.

4. Bronko Nagurski.

5. Willie Davis.

6. Don Hutson.

7. Pete Rozelle.

8. Otto Graham.

9. Joe Montana.

10. Hank Stram.

EXTRA POINT

"There are three important things in life; family, religion and the Green Bay Packers."

-Super Bowl coaching legend *Vince Lombardi*

THE SIXTIES

1. Before the American Football League and the National Football League merged, the upstart AFL began play in 1960. How many of the eight original teams can you name?

2. Who did Green Bay defeat in 1967 to earn the right to represent the NFL against the AFL's Chiefs?

3. Who did the Packers beat in the "Ice Bowl" in '67 to allow them to defend their NFL championship?

4. Name the *Monday Night Football* announcer and Pro Football Hall of Famer who was a television analyst in the first Super Bowl.

5. Do you know the 1963 Heisman Trophy winner who played in the Super Bowl?

6. What Super Bowl II's defensive team was called "Eleven Angry Men?"

7. Who was the coach of Green Bay's two Super Bowl-winning teams of the '60s?

8. What 1968 Super Bowl team played against the Jets in the infamous "Heidi" game?

9. Who was the first coach to win titles in both the NFL and the AFL?

10. In 1968, the Houston Oilers left Rice Stadium to play in the Astrodome, thus becoming the first team to play its home games in a domed stadium. In all, how many Super Bowls were played in the Astrodome?

ANSWERS

1. The Boston Patriots, Buffalo Bills, Dallas Texans, Denver Broncos, Houston Oilers, L.A. Chargers, New York Titans and Oakland Raiders.

2. The Dallas Cowboys, 34-27.

3. Again, the Dallas Cowboys, 21-17.

4. Frank Gifford.

5. Roger Staubach.

6. The Raiders.

7. Vince Lombardi.

8. The Raiders … In a regular season game, NBC opted to cut out the last 50 seconds of the contest in order to begin the children's special at its regular time. The Raiders went on to score two touchdowns in the last 42 seconds to beat the Jets, 43-32.

9. Weeb Ewbank.

10. 0.

EXTRA POINT

"He'll be the first quarterback in history to play three quarters and be able to bill them for four."

-*Jay Leno*, about *Steve Young* going to law school

TOUCH TONE TRIVIA

See if you can solve the clues below using the telephone touch pad's assistance. Each player's last name is spelled numerically. Example: FAULK is 32855 (F falls in DEF or "3" range, A in ABC or 2, etc.).

1. 6655 is the only head coach to win four Super Bowls.

2. 52967754 quarterbacked the Eagles in their only Super Bowl appearance.

3. 786637255 retired from play by play duties after Super Bowl XXXVI.

4. 25536 has the longest run from scrimmage in Super Bowl history, 74 yards.

5. 645536 played with three different Super Bowl winning teams.

6. 74852 is one of three coaches to have four Super Bowl losses.

7. 627846 intercepted three passes against Philadelphia in 1981.

8. 5233 sang the national anthem in Super Bowl XII and was one of "Charlie's Angels".

9. 829567 was the first player to score a rushing touchdown in a Super Bowl.

10. 24747843 kicked the longest field goal in Super Bowl history, 54 yards.

ANSWERS

1. Chuck Noll.

2. Ron Jaworski.

3. Pat Summerall.

4. Marcus Allen.

5. Matt Millen (Raiders, 49ers and Redskins).

6. Don Shula (1969 with Baltimore and in '72, '83, and '85 with Miami).

7. Rod Martin.

8. Cheryl Ladd.

9. Jim Taylor.

10. Steve Christie.

EXTRA POINT

"Sure, we're in limos - we're stars.
How else is a star supposed to travel?"

- **Deion Sanders**, on traveling around town in limousines before the Cowboys game against the Steelers in Super Bowl XXX

YOUR NUMBER'S UP

Match the Super Bowl player with his retired jersey number.

1. John Elway	a)	19
2. Lawrence Taylor	b)	70
3. Bart Starr	c)	16
4. Isaac Bruce	d)	7
5. Johnny Unitas	e)	56
6. Jack Youngblood	f)	34
7. Jim Marshall	g)	80
8. Bob Griese	h)	85
9. Walter Payton	i)	15
10. Joe Montana	j)	12

EXTRA POINT

"I'm a 'Save the Whales' guy."

-Giants general manager and architect of two
Super Bowl winners, ***George Young***,
explaining why he likes offensive linemen

ANSWERS

1. D.

2. E.

3. I.

4. G.

5. A.

6. H.

7. B.

8. J.

9. F.

10. C.

EXTRA POINT

"If me and King Kong went into an alley, only one of us would come out, and it wouldn't be the monkey."

- *Lyle Alzado*, defensive lineman of the Super Bowl XII Broncos

A SIMPLE SUPER BOWL YES OR NO WILL DO

1. Does the winning team get to keep the Super Bowl trophy?

2. Did Jim Brown ever play in a Super Bowl?

3. Has there ever been a shutout?

4. Has any player ever caught three touchdown passes in a game?

5. Has there ever been an overtime game?

6. Has any team ever won three consecutive Super Bowls?

7. Did any team score more than 50 points in a game?

8. Has any team played in more than 5 Super Bowls?

9. Was Pete Rozelle the NFL commissioner at the first Super Bowl?

10. Was the Cotton Bowl ever the site for a Super Bowl?

EXTRA POINT

"My mom says it's because I don't shave."

-Two-time Super Bowl champion *Brett Favre*,
on why he doesn't get as many commercial
endorsements as fellow quarterback *Troy Aikman*

ANSWERS

1. Yes.

2. No.

3. No.

4. Yes (Jerry Rice, San Francisco, XXIV).

5. No.

6. No.

7. Yes (Dallas, XXVII and San Francisco, XXIV).

8. Yes (Dallas 8 and Denver 6).

9. Yes.

10. No.

EXTRA POINT

"Don't blame me. Blame the foursome ahead of me."

-*Lawrence Taylor*, when late for a Giants practice

STADIA MANIA

1. What stadium's address is Super Bowl Drive?

2. Super Bowls II and III were hosted in the same stadium. Do you know it?

3. In what stadium was the first Super Bowl to be played north of the Mason-Dixon line?

4. Super Bowl XXXII was played in Qualcomm Stadium. What was the venue originally called?

5. Name the only Super Bowl site to also host a World Series and an NCAA Final Four basketball tournament.

6. Four Super Bowl sites have also been the home of a big league baseball team. How many can you think of?

7. The largest attendance at a Super Bowl was 103,985. Where was the game played?

8. What was Pro Player Stadium, site of three Super Bowls, originally called?

9. Has a team ever played at a Super Bowl site which was also its home during the regular season?

10. The big game has been played at four different sites in California. The Los Angeles Coliseum, Qualcomm Stadium and the Rose Bowl are three. Can you name the fourth?

ANSWERS

1. The Superdome in New Orleans.

2. Miami's Orange Bowl.

3. The Pontiac (Michigan) Silverdome, XVI.

4. Jack Murphy Stadium (in San Diego).

5. Minnesota's Metrodome (XXVI).

6. San Diego's Qualcomm Stadium (Padres), Miami's Pro Player Stadium (Marlins), Minnesota's Metrodome (Twins) and the Los Angeles Memorial Coliseum (Dodgers played there from 1959-'62 until Dodger Stadium was completed).

7. The Rose Bowl (Raiders and Vikings, XI).

8. Joe Robbie Stadium.

9. No.

10. Stanford Stadium (XIX).

EXTRA POINT

"If it's the ultimate game,
how come they're playing it again next year?"

- ***Tony Dorsett***, on the Super Bowl

A RUSH ORDER

1. What running back played for the Packers in Super Bowls I and II and had his uniform number retired by the New Orleans Saints?

2. Can you name the Super Bowl running back whose son became an All-NBA first team member?

3. In Super Bowl VIII he became the first running back to be named MVP. Name him.

4. Do you know the only player to rush for over 100 yards and average more than 10 yards per carry in a Super Bowl game?

5. Name the player who rushed for 135 yards in a losing effort against the Giants in 1991.

6. After the Redskins beat the Dolphins, 27-17 in Super Bowl XVII, who said, "Reagan may be president, but today I'm king"?

7. Did Earl Campbell ever play in a Super Bowl?

8. Did Walter Payton ever score a Super Bowl touchdown?

9. Which back ran for a Super Bowl record 204 yards in the Redskins 42-10 drubbing of the Broncos?

10. Who scored the Jets only touchdown in Super Bowl III?

ANSWERS

1. Jim Taylor.

2. Calvin Hill (father of Grant).

3. Larry Csonka.

4. Tom Matte, Colts vs. Jets, 1969, 11 carries, 116 yards.

5. Thurman Thomas of the Bills.

6. John Riggins.

7. No.

8. No.

9. Timmy Smith (XXII).

10. Matt Snell.

EXTRA POINT

"The Bears aren't very genteel.
Some teams tend to remove the football from you.
The Bears remove you from the football. It's quicker."

-*Jim Murray*, about the 1986 (XX)
championship Bears team

PIGSKIN POTPOURRI

1. What two teams are each 0-4 in Super Bowl play?

2. Name two quarterbacks with the initials "T.B." who have won the Super Bowl MVP Award.

3. What team was the first to win five Super Bowls?

4. Who is the only quarterback to play in five Super Bowls?

5. Who's the only player to be a part of three consecutive Super Bowl titles?

6. Can you name the only Super Bowl MVP to become an NFL head coach?

7. The Dallas Texans relocated and became known as what Super Bowl team?

8. Who has coached in the most Super Bowl games?

9. Do you know who coined the term "Super Bowl?"

10. What Tennessee Titan became the second half of the first father-son combination to start in a Super Bowl game?

EXTRA POINT

"Losing the Super Bowl is worse than death.
You have to get up the next morning."

- George Allen

ANSWERS

1. Buffalo and Minnesota.

2. Tom Brady and Terry Bradshaw.

3. The San Francisco 49ers.

4. John Elway.

5. Ken Norton Jr., with the Cowboys in XXVII and XXVIII and with the 49ers in XXIX.

6. Bart Starr.

7. The Kansas City Chiefs.

8. Don Shula, 6 times (Baltimore, 1969; Miami, 1972, '73, '74, '83 and '85).

9. K.C. Chiefs owner Lamar Hunt.

10. Free safety Anthony Dorsett (XXXIV) whose father, Tony, started for the Cowboys in Super Bowls XII and XIII.

EXTRA POINT

"I'm probably about a 4.9 normally, but when a 280-pound guy is chasing me, I'm a 4.6."

-*John Elway*, on his speed in the 40-yard dash

WHO AM I?

1. I was the first African-American to quarterback in the Super Bowl.

2. I was the first defensive player to score in the Super Bowl, returning an interception 60 yards for a touchdown in 1968.

3. A backup quarterback, I'm the only player to be on five consecutive Super Bowl teams.

4. Although I'm a defensive tackle, I rushed for a touchdown in Super Bowl XX.

5. I recorded three sacks to set a Super Bowl record against New England in 1997.

6. I've thrown the most completed passes in Super Bowl history.

7. I'm the only player to be with five Super Bowl winners.

8. Harvey Martin and I are the only players to be named NFL defensive player of the year and Super Bowl MVP in the same season.

9. I threw for a Super Bowl-record 414 yards against the Titans.

10. I intercepted two passes in Super Bowl XXX to help the Cowboys beat the Steelers, 27-17.

ANSWERS

1. Doug Williams.

2. Herb Adderley.

3. Gale Gilbert ... Gilbert was on the Bills roster for the 1991-'94 Super Bowls and was with the Chargers in 1995.

4. William "Refrigerator" Perry.

5. Reggie White.

6. Joe Montana, 83.

7. Charles Haley.

8. Ray Lewis.

9. Kurt Warner.

10. Larry Brown.

EXTRA POINT

"If I'm sleeping, how will I know what kind of good time somebody is having without me?"

-John Matuszak, complaining about having to go to sleep early the night before a Super Bowl game

TEAMING UP

1. Name the only team to win the Super Bowl back to back twice.

2. The highest point total for two teams in a single Super Bowl is 75, occurring in Super Bowl XXIX. Do you know the teams?

3. Only one Super Bowl was tied at the half, 3-3 in 1989. What were the teams?

4. Dick Vermeil has coached two teams in the Super Bowl. One was the Rams. How about the other?

5. Cowboys coach Tom Landry is credited with giving the "No Name Defense" moniker to the defensive unit of what team?

6. What 1993 Super Bowl team turned the ball over a record nine times?

7. After losing Super Bowl V in their blue jerseys, what team developed a superstition about their uniforms?

8. In 2002, what team chose to be introduced as a "team" rather than as individual starters on offense or defense?

9. Do you know the only two teams to meet each other in the Super Bowl three times?

10. Joe Kapp was a losing quarterback on what Super Bowl team?

ANSWERS

1. Pittsburgh.

2. The 49ers and Chargers ... San Francisco won, 49-26.

3. The 49ers and Bengals.

4. Philadelphia.

5. Miami.

6. The Buffalo Bills.

7. Dallas ... To this day, road opponents often force the Cowboys to play in blue rather than the usual visiting whites.

8. New England, to symbolize the team effort that had gotten the over-achieving Patriots to the Super Bowl.

9. Dallas and Pittsburgh (X, XIII and XXX).

10. The Minnesota Vikings.

EXTRA POINT

"I think all uniforms look nice
if you've got good players in 'em."

-*Bill Parcells*, coach of Giants and Patriots Super Bowl teams

FOUR-LETTER MEN

The answers to all of these clues are four-letter last names.

1. He coached an AFC East team in four Super Bowls.

2. An offensive lineman, he's appeared more than once in a Super Bowl and was the NFL's overall #1 pick in 1997.

3. He was the coach of the Bears 46 defense in Super Bowl XX.

4. He made four Super Bowl appearances, was one of the "Purple People Eaters" and today is on the Minneapolis Supreme Court.

5. A footballer turned broadcaster, this defensive lineman was a member of the Super Bowl Raiders.

6. He recovered and returned placekicker Garo Yepremian's fumble in Super Bowl VII for a touchdown.

7. He kicked the winning field goal for the Giants in their 20-19 win over the Bills.

8. He was named MVP when the Bears downed the Patriots, 46-10.

9. This linebacker wore number 78 and played with the Kansas City Chiefs his entire career, including their Super Bowl years in 1967 and '70.

10. He's the owner of the Super Bowl IV winners.

ANSWERS

1. Marv Levy.

2. Orlando Pace.

3. Buddy Ryan.

4. Alan Page.

5. Howie Long.

6. Mike Bass.

7. Matt Bahr.

8. Richard Dent.

9. Bobby Bell.

10. Lamar Hunt.

EXTRA POINT

"That's impossible. It takes him 12 hours to comb his hair."

- *Jerry Glanville*, about Cowboys Super Bowl coach
Jimmy Johnson's claim that he works 18 hours a day.

THE SEVENTIES

1. Name the 1987 and 1991 Super Bowl-winning team which played its final Yankee Stadium home game in 1973, tying the Eagles 23-23.

2. Do you know the Baltimore Colts receiver who scored on a 75-yard pass from Johnny Unitas in Super Bowl V against the Cowboys?

3. Who were the opposing quarterbacks when Miami defeated Washington, 14-7, in 1973?

4. The Steelers won back to back Super Bowls in 1975 and 1976. Who did they beat?

5. Three Super Bowls (V, X and XIII) were played at this stadium in the seventies. Do you know it?

6. Who was the first lefthanded quarterback to win a Super Bowl?

7. What team played in five Super Bowls with a record of 2-3 in the seventies?

8. In 1979, what team became the first to win three Super Bowls?

9. Who kicked three field goals, the first scores of the game, when the Chiefs upset the Vikings in Super Bowl IV in 1970?

10. What team was denied going to the Super Bowl when they lost five AFC Championship games in the seventies?

ANSWERS

1. The New York Giants.

2. John Mackey.

3. Bob Griese (Dolphins) and Billy Kilmer (Redskins).

4. The Vikings and Cowboys.

5. The Orange Bowl.

6. Ken Stabler, when the Raiders defeated the Vikings, 32-14, in 1977.

7. The Cowboys.

8. The Steelers.

9. Jan Stenerud.

10. The Raiders.

EXTRA POINT

"I don't like it. Now I have to pay taxes in three states."

-Kansas City Chiefs linebacker **Buddy Bell**, a resident of Minnesota, on Super Bowl I being held in California

EITHER OR

Decide which of the following choices is the correct answer.

1. He was the first coach to take two different NFL teams to the Super Bowl. Was it Don Shula or Bill Parcells?

2. They are the only team to go to at least six Super Bowls and face six different opponents. Is it the Broncos or the Cowboys?

3. They were the first team with a bird nickname to win the Super Bowl. Was it the Ravens or the Eagles?

4. The Super Bowl MVP receives the Vince Lombardi or the Pete Rozelle Trophy?

5. A field goal was this team's lone score in one Super Bowl contest. Was it the Dolphins or the Patriots?

6. The NFC's streak of 13 Super Bowl wins was broken by this team on January 25, 1998. Was it the Broncos or the Steelers?

7. He was the only man to start on both offense and defense in a Super Bowl. Was it E.J. Holub or Deion Sanders?

8. The first man to kick four field goals in a Super Bowl was Jan Stenerud or Don Chandler?

9. The Heisman Trophy's only two-time winner played in Super Bowl XVI. Was it Archie Griffin or Joe Theismann?

10. He completed 22 out of 25 passes for a Super Bowl-record completion of 88%. Was it Joe Montana or Phil Simms?

ANSWERS

1. Don Shula … He led the Baltimore Colts and Miami Dolphins to Super Bowls.

2. The Broncos … They've played the Cowboys, Giants, Redskins, 49ers, Packers and the Falcons.

3. The Ravens.

4. The Pete Rozelle Trophy.

5. Miami (in Super Bowl VI against Dallas).

6. The Broncos, 31-24 over the Packers.

7. E.J. Holub … He started at linebacker for the Chiefs in Super Bowl I and at center in Super Bowl IV. Sanders saw action in Super Bowl XXX as both wide receiver and cornerback but did not start at both positions.

8. Don Chandler, in Super Bowl II.

9. Archie Griffin … Despite the fact that he changed the pronunciation of his last name to rhyme with Heisman, Joe Theismann never won the award.

10. Phil Simms.

EXTRA POINT

"John Elway is the master of the inconceivable pass to the unreachable spot."

- Super Bowl announcer *Pat Summerall*

ALMA MATER

Match the Super Bowl quarterback with the college he attended.

1. Terry Bradshaw	a) Northern Iowa
2. Tom Brady	b) UCLA
3. Steve McNair	c) Stanford
4. Kurt Warner	d) Miami
5. Brett Favre	e) Louisiana Tech
6. Jim Plunkett	f) Purdue
7. Troy Aikman	g) Southern Mississippi
8. Jim Kelly	h) Brigham Young
9. Jim McMahon	i) Alcorn State
10. Len Dawson	j) Michigan

EXTRA POINT

"Go and ask Henderson if I was dumb today."

-Steelers quarterback and Super Bowl XIII MVP *Terry Bradshaw*. Before the game *Thomas* "Hollywood" *Henderson* had called Bradshaw "dumb," saying, Bradshaw couldn't spell "cat" if you spotted him the "c" and the "a."

ANSWERS

1. E.

2. J.

3. I.

4. A.

5. G.

6. C.

7. B.

8. D.

9. H.

10. F.

EXTRA POINT

"You know, at the circus - they bring those little cars in and 18 guys get out. He'd be in that group."

*-**Bill Parcells**, on 5'8" Stephen Baker, wide receiver on the Super Bowl XXV Giants*

PASSING FADS

*Listed below are the last names of quarterback/receiver combos,
all of whom have teamed up for at least one Super Bowl touchdown.
The letters are in their proper order, but the names have
been combined. Your job is to separate them.*

Example - WBRARUNECRE = Warner and Bruce.

1. OT'DHONINEGPELNL

2. AIIRKVMIANN

3. YWAOTUTENRGS

4. SBAIMVAMROS

5. FFAREEVMAREN

6. BSRAWDSANHNAW

7. MROINTCANEA

8. BCOLAEDTSEOSE

9. PBLURNKANECTHT

10. SDOTAWLERRR

EXTRA POINT

"A stick of gum would have been enough."

-Raiders wide receiver ***Fred Biletnikoff***,
as he held his Super Bowl XI MVP trophy

ANSWERS

1. O'Donnell and Thigpen.

2. Aikman and Irvin.

3. Young and Watters.

4. Simms and Bavaro.

5. Favre and Freeman.

6. Bradshaw and Swann.

7. Montana and Rice.

8. Bledsoe and Coates.

9. Plunkett and Branch.

10. Starr and Dowler.

EXTRA POINT

"They're married to them."

-*Forrest Gregg*, on why he permitted Bengals players
to sleep with their wives before the Super Bowl

WHO YOU TALKIN' 'BOUT?

See if you know the Super Bowler (player, coach, etc.) they're talking about. We've clued you in on the team they represent.

1. "If _____ was a general, he would be able to overrun Europe with the army from Sweden." (49ers) -***Beano Cook***

2. "It's like he runs with snow tires and everybody else on the field has sneakers." (Bills) -***Dave Adolph***

3. "Everybody knows he's coming. It's like a cop putting sirens on his car." (Giants) -***Beasley Reece***

4. "Jerry wants a lot of things. In fact, Jerry wants everything." (Cowboys) -***Jimmy Johnson***

5. "Why, Jack's so mean he doesn't even like himself." (Steelers) -***Joe Greene***

6. "Coach _____ is very fair. He treats us all like dogs." (Packers) -***Henry Jordan***

7. "Give that man just a crease and he's something special. He can stop on a dime and give you nine and a half cents change. (Cowboys) -***Nate Newton***

8. "I don't know if he'll be there with us in the Hall of Fame. Hell, they might have to build this boy his own wing." (49ers) -***Sammy Baugh***

9. "His pedigree was super. He was by Paul Brown out of Sid Gillman by Don Shula." (Steelers) -***Art Rooney***

10. "I spent 12 years training for a career that was over in a week. _____ spent one week for a career that lasted 12 years." (Jets) -***Bruce Jenner***, Olympic decathlon gold medalist

ANSWERS

1. Bill Walsh.

2. Thurman Thomas.

3. Lawrence Taylor.

4. Jerry Jones.

5. Jack Lambert.

6. Vince Lombardi.

7. Emmitt Smith.

8. Joe Montana.

9. Chuck Noll.

10. Joe Namath.

EXTRA POINT

"Concentration-wise, we're having trouble
crossing the line from a toughness standpoint."

-Bill Parcells

FOR THE RECORD

1. When Rams quarterback Kurt Warner passed for 414 yards against the Titans in 2000, whose record did he break?

2. What player has scored the most Super Bowl points?

3. Who's the all-time leading Super Bowl rusher?

4. What ignominious distinction do Bud Grant, Don Shula, Marv Levy and Dan Reeves share?

5. What team has played in the most Super Bowls?

6. In 1992, what quarterback threw 58 passes to set the record for most attempts in a game?

7. What running back set the record (since tied) for most points in a game, 18? Hint: he did it against Miami in 1985.

8. Joe Montana holds the all-time record for TD passes with 11. Who's second?

9. This Cowboys quarterback played in four Super Bowls and fumbled a record five times. Name him.

10. The 49ers have the winningest record in Super Bowl history, 5-0. Three other teams are undefeated in Super Bowl play. Do you know them?

ANSWERS

1. Joe Montana's (357 yards vs. the Bengals in 1989).

2. Jerry Rice, 42.

3. Franco Harris, 354 yards.

4. Each has coached four losing Super Bowl teams.

5. Dallas, 8.

6. Jim Kelly of the Bills … He completed 28 of the 58.

7. San Francisco's Roger Craig.

8. Terry Bradshaw, 9.

9. Roger Staubach.

10. The Jets, Bears and Ravens are all 1-0.

EXTRA POINT

"Paul Hornung was an impact player for the Packers. He was also an impact player to half the females in the USA."

-*Max McGee*, a member of the Super Bowl I Packers, talking about his teammate

LAUGH-IN TIME-OUT

It's time to take a trivia breather with these groaners about the game.

Muggsy and Buggsy had been together in Hell for many, many years. Their eternal job was to shovel coal into the fires side by side.

Suddenly, one day they felt cold air. The air got colder and colder. Snow began to fall. The next thing they knew, there was a blizzard. The snow blanketed the ground and extinguished the fires. Next, a gust of wind froze over the entire surface of Hell!

"What the heck is going on here?" Muggsy wondered out loud.

Buggsy answered, "I don't know for sure, but I have a hunch that the Bills just won the Super Bowl."

Q: What do you call a New Orleans Saint with a Super Bowl ring?

A: Thief

EXTRA POINT

"Hey, Norm, isn't he one of ours?"

-Green Bay quarterback ***Bart Starr***, to Super Bowl I referee ***Norm Schachter***, when he found out that one of the three NFL officials (working with three AFL officials) had called a penalty against the Packers

LAUGH-IN TIME-OUT
(CONTINUED)

A guy desperately wants to go to the Super Bowl so he finds a scalper but can get only one ticket. He pays top dollar for a seat in the nosebleed section, the second to last row of the upper deck. As the game begins, the guy's watching through his binoculars. He notices that there's an empty seat in the very first row, right on the fifty yard line. As the second quarter is about to end, he looks down and sees that the fifty yard line seat is still empty. At halftime, he makes his way down to the empty seat and asks the guy who's sitting in the next seat, "Is this taken?"

The guy replies, "No."

"Well then, would you mind if I sit here?"

The other guy says, "Not at all. Go right ahead."

"I wonder why someone with a front row, fifty yard line seat wouldn't show up at the Super Bowl," says the first guy.

The second guy says, "Actually, my wife and I have come to every Super Bowl since 1967, but she passed away."

"Oh, gee, I'm sorry to hear that," says the first guy. "But couldn't you get a friend or relative to come to the game?"

"They're all at the funeral."

EXTRA POINT

"Eight beers and two hours' sleep a night."

-*Pete Banaszak*, on Raiders quarterback *Ken Stabler*
(Super Bowl II) and how he prepares for a game

ON THE ROAD
TO THE SUPER BOWL

See if you can answer these postseason questions.

1. Since the Super Bowl began, there has been only one NFC Championship sudden death overtime game. Can you name the teams and the outcome?

2. In 1986, the Broncos defeated the Browns in overtime, 23-20, for the AFC title. What was John Elway's march down the field called?

3. In the 1982 NFC Championship, Dwight Clark caught a TD pass, giving the 49ers a 28-27 win over the Cowboys. The play is simply known as what?

4. "The Immaculate Reception" was a fourth down, fourth quarter desperation pass from Steeler quarterback Terry Bradshaw to whom?

5. The longest game in NFL history took place in an AFC divisional playoff contest in 1971. Who played and what was the result?

6. Two teams have won six AFC title games (including AFL Championships). Can you name either one?

7. What team has played in the most AFC Championship games, 12, but has a losing record of 4-8?

8. In a 1992 AFC Wild Card game, Warren Moon staked the Oilers to a 35-3 lead, but the Bills mounted the greatest comeback in history, winning in overtime, 41-38. Name the Buffalo quarterback who threw four TD passes in the second half.

9. The Rams were shut out by the Cowboys, 28-0, in the 1978 NFC Championship but turned the tables the next year when they shut out what opponent, 9-0?

10. Can you name the 49ers running back who set a one game postseason best with five touchdowns against the Giants in a 1993 divisional clash?

ANSWERS

1. Atlanta defeated Minnesota, 30-27, in 1998.

2. "The Drive."

3. "The Catch."

4. Franco Harris … The pass, intended for Frenchy Fuqua, was misthrown but miraculously wound up in Harris' hands, giving the Steelers a 13-7 AFC divisional playoff win over the Raiders in 1972.

5. Miami defeated Kansas City when Garo Yepremian kicked a 37-yard field goal more than 22 minutes into overtime to give the Dolphins a 27-24 victory.

6. The Bills and Broncos.

7. The Raiders.

8. Frank Reich.

9. Tampa Bay.

10. Ricky Watters.

EXTRA POINT

"I had frog legs for my appetizer.
That's why I'm so jumpy this morning."

-*Nate Newton*, on Super Bowl game day

GETTING THEIR KICKS

1. Whose five field goals accounted for all of the Giants scoring, enabling them to advance to the Super Bowl after their 15-13 win in the 1990 NFC title game against the 49ers?

2. What placekicker missed a 47-yard field goal to allow the Giants a 20-19 win over the Bills in Super Bowl XXV?

3. This Bengal owns the Super Bowl record for the longest punt, 63 yards, against the 49ers in 1989. Name him.

4. Has a placekicker ever been selected as Super Bowl MVP?

5. Has a punt/kickoff returner ever been chosen as the MVP?

6. Who kicked a 48-yard field goal as time expired to give the Patriots the win over the Rams, 20-17, in 2002?

7. Has a punt ever been returned for a touchdown in a Super Bowl?

8. The Miami Dolphins were held to just one field goal in a 24-3 Super Bowl loss to the Cowboys. Who scored Miami's only points?

9. The Giants only touchdown in their 34-7 loss to the Ravens in Super Bowl XXXV came on a 97-yard kickoff return by what player?

10. Do you know the Cowboy kicker who booted the most punts in a single Super Bowl game? Hint: his initials are R.W. … hint, hint … it was against the Colts in 1971.

ANSWERS

1. Matt Bahr's.

2. Scott Norwood.

3. Lee Johnson.

4. No.

5. Yes ... Desmond Howard in Super Bowl XXXI.

6. Adam Vinatieri.

7. No.

8. Garo Yepremian.

9. Ron Dixon.

10. Ron Widby.

EXTRA POINT

"It's a good thing William (The Refrigerator) Perry doesn't need it. They'd have had to use a harpoon."

-*Buddy Baron*, talking about Jim McMahon's acupuncture prior to Super Bowl XX

KEEPING SCORE

Match the Super Bowl teams with the final score.

1. Chiefs over Vikings (IV)	a)	27-17
2. Dolphins over Vikings (VIII)	b)	30-13
3. Cowboys over Broncos (XII)	c)	23-7
4. Steelers over Rams (XIV)	d)	46-10
5. Redskins over Dolphins (XVII)	e)	32-24
6. Raiders over Redskins (XVIII)	f)	24-7
7. Bears over Patriots (XX)	g)	34-19
8. Redskins over Bills (XXVI)	h)	27-10
9. Cowboys over Bills (XXVIII)	i)	38-9
10. Broncos over Falcons (XXXIII)	j)	31-19

EXTRA POINT

"When we go to a party, the hostess is still in the shower."

-Mrs. Vince Lombardi, on the coach's punctuality

ANSWERS

1. C.

2. F.

3. H.

4. J.

5. A.

6. I.

7. D.

8. E.

9. B.

10. G.

EXTRA POINT

"A good coach needs three things: a patient wife, a loyal dog and a great quarterback - not necessarily in that order."

-Bud Grant

PIGSKIN POTPOURRI

1. What was the first Super Bowl to be played in the month of February?

2. Which came first, the inaugural Super Bowl or ABC's *Monday Night Football*?

3. The winning quarterback in Super Bowls VI through XIV wore what number?

4. The Chicago Bears cut the first sports music video in the 1980s. What was it called?

5. Name the first team to play its home games in a domed stadium and then go on to win a Super Bowl.

6. Who's the only player to be named Super Bowl MVP three times?

7. This kicker has booted field goals in two different Super Bowls and shares the record for the longest field goal in NFL history - 63 yards. Name him.

8. Of all the Super Bowl participants who are enshrined in the Pro Football Hall of Fame, who is listed first alphabetically?

9. Two outdoor venues have hosted the Super Bowl five times. Can you name them?

10. Who was the first man to play in a major league baseball game and in a Super Bowl game?

ANSWERS

1. XXXVI between the Patriots and Rams, won by New England, 20-17.

2. The first Super Bowl (January 15, 1967) … *Monday Night Football* made its debut in 1970.

3. 12.

4. *The Super Bowl Shuffle.*

5. The St. Louis Rams.

6. Joe Montana.

7. Jason Elam.

8. Herb Adderley of the Green Bay Packers … He's also the first alphabetically, period.

9. The Rose Bowl and the Orange Bowl.

10. Tom Brown (for the baseball Washington Senators and the football Green Bay Packers).

EXTRA POINT

"If I didn't enjoy gloating so much,
I probably wouldn't do as many interviews."

-Cowboys coach *Jimmy Johnson*

THE EIGHTIES

1. What team lost two consecutive Super Bowls in the eighties?

2. The CBS telecast of Super Bowl XVI in 1982 achieved the highest rating of any televised sports event ever, 49.1 with a 73.0 share. Who were the participants?

3. When a team relocated to it in 1984, this stadium could lay claim to being the home of two Super Bowl winners. Do you know the facility?

4. What head coach won three Super Bowls in the eighties?

5. Do you know the Super Bowl team of the eighties which has retired the most uniform numbers in NFL history?

6. What network telecast its first Super Bowl, a 49ers-Dolphins game, in 1985?

7. In 1986, Chicago's Mike Ditka became the second man to win a Super Bowl ring as a player and a coach. Who was first?

8. Who's the only wide receiver to win a Super Bowl MVP award in the eighties?

9. In 1982, the NFL adopted a format of 16 teams competing in a Super Bowl Tournament for the playoffs. How come?

10. What team has scored the fewest total points in Super Bowl games?

ANSWERS

1. The Broncos, against the Giants in '87 and the Redskins in '88.

2. San Francisco and Cincinnati (49ers won, 26-21).

3. Giants Stadium, home to the Giants since 1976, and to the Jets since 1984.

4. San Francisco's Bill Walsh.

5. The Chicago Bears, 13.

6. ABC.

7. Tom Flores of the Raiders.

8. Jerry Rice of the 49ers, in 1989.

9. Because the regular season was reduced from a 16-game schedule to nine as the result of a 57-day players' strike.

10. Philadelphia … The Eagles appeared in just one Super Bowl (1981) and were beaten by the Raiders, 27-10.

EXTRA POINT

"The question is: Is Bourbon Street ready for me?"

-Bears quarterback *Jim McMahon*, when asked before Super Bowl XX in New Orleans if he was prepared for Bourbon Street

THE HALL OF NAMES

Identify the Super Bowl participant from his nickname.

Nickname	Super Bowl(s)
1. Sweetness	XX
2. Minister of Defense	XXXI, XXXII
3. The Artful Dodger	VI, X, XII, XIII
4. The Polish Rifle	XV
5. Snake	XI
6. Touchdown Tony	XII, XIII
7. Ozark Ike	IX, X, XIII, XIV
8. The Scrambler	VIII, IX, XI
9. Tuna	XXI, XXV, XXXI
10. Broadway Joe	III

EXTRA POINT

"The game of football is Xs and Os.
In their case, it should be O and X, which spells Ox."

-*Hank Stram*, on the huge offensive line of the
Super Bowl XXX winners, the Dallas Cowboys

ANSWERS

1. Walter Payton.

2. Reggie White.

3. Roger Staubach.

4. Ron Jaworski.

5. Ken Stabler.

6. Tony Dorsett.

7. Terry Bradshaw.

8. Fran Tarkenton.

9. Bill Parcells.

10. Joe Namath.

EXTRA POINT

"My job has become decoy. I draw the attack and the other guys make the plays. I should show up painted like a duck."

-*Howie Long*, defensive lineman for the 1984 Super Bowl Raiders

ON THE JOHN

Who are these "Johns?"

1. A defensive back for the 1958 and '59 championship Colt teams, he was also a member of the Super Bowl-winning Jets in 1969.

2. He ran for 166 yards on 38 carries to spark the Redskins to a 27-17 win over the Dolphins in Super Bowl XVII.

3. The number one pick of the Colts in the 1983 draft, he never played a down for them. Hint: he was on back to back Super Bowl winners.

4. He has the best winning percentage of any coach with more than 100 NFL victories and led his team to a win in Super Bowl XI.

5. He quarterbacked in Super Bowls III and V and was named to the NFL's 75th anniversary all-time team.

6. A 49ers wide receiver, he played on three Super Bowl winners.

7. He caught two touchdown passes in Super Bowl XIII as the Steelers upended the Cowboys, 35-31.

8. One of the game's greatest guards, he retired a year before his team, the Patriots, made it to the Super Bowl.

9. He was a standout tight end for the Colts and played in Super Bowl III against the Jets.

10. This San Diego placekicker scored 135 regular season points in 1994 and played in Super Bowl XXIX against the 49ers.

ANSWERS

1. Johnny Sample.

2. John Riggins.

3. John Elway.

4. John Madden.

5. Johnny Unitas.

6. John Taylor.

7. John Stallworth.

8. John Hannah.

9. John Mackey.

10. John Carney.

EXTRA POINT

"We hitched our wagon to a Starr."

-*Jim Taylor*, about the Super Bowl leadership
of Green Bay's **Bart Starr**

THE NAME GAME

See if you can decipher the Super Bowl team by its description.

Team	Super Bowl(s)
1. Royal Birds	XXXIII
2. Mountain Dwellers	XIV, XXXIV, XXXVI
3. Seven Squared	XVI, XIX, XXIII, XXIV, XXIX
4. Debits	XXV, XXVI, XXVII, XXVIII
5. Poe's Birds	XXXV
6. Visa Experts	XXIX
7. Minute Men	XX, XXXI, XXXVI
8. Tribe Elders	I, IV
9. Lilliput Adversaries	XXI, XXV, XXXV
10. Rash Results	VII, XVII, XVIII, XXII, XXVI

EXTRA POINT

"Orange Crush is soda water, baby.
You drink it. It don't win football games."

-**Harvey Martin**, after the 1980 Super Bowl in which the
Cowboys beat the Broncos - nicknamed the Orange Crush

ANSWERS

1. Falcons.

2. Rams.

3. 49ers.

4. Bills.

5. Ravens.

6. Chargers.

7. Patriots.

8. Chiefs.

9. Giants.

10. Redskins.

EXTRA POINT

"We're as clean as any team.
We wash our hands before we hit anybody."

-*Nate Newton*, answering claims
that the Cowboys were a dirty team

THE ONE AND ONLY

1. Who's the only player to appear in the Super Bowl in three different decades?

2. Can you name the only Super Bowl team to play its home games in New York?

3. Who's the only Super Bowl MVP to become an NFL head coach?

4. What Super Bowl player is the only placekicker in the Hall of Fame?

5. In quarterback Dan Marino's only Super Bowl appearance, the Dolphins lost to what team?

6. Who's the only man to rush for three touchdowns in a Super Bowl?

7. Who's the only coach to win four Super Bowls?

8. What's the only Super Bowl that wasn't a sellout?

9. For what unusual reason did Super Bowl I become the only such game to start the second half with two kickoffs?

10. Name the only team to re-locate, and as a result, win Super Bowls representing more than one city.

ANSWERS

1. Gene Upshaw - 1968, 1977 and 1981.

2. The Buffalo Bills (The Giants and Jets both play their home games in East Rutherford, N.J.).

3. Bart Starr.

4. Jan Stenerud.

5. San Francisco.

6. Terrell Davis, in Super Bowl XXXII when Denver bested Green Bay, 31-24.

7. Chuck Noll.

8. Super Bowl I.

9. NBC was airing a commercial and missed the first one. Officials nullified that kickoff and had the half start over again.

10. The Raiders (Oakland and Los Angeles).

EXTRA POINT

"It's too soon after the car wreck to say we're feeling better."

-Bills coach ***Marv Levy***, meeting with his team
after their fourth straight Super Bowl loss

HALFTIME

1. What computer company launched an ad during the 1984 Super Bowl that many advertising afficionados consider to be the best ever created?

2. This 1989 series of commercials was the first of annual matchups featuring "light" vs. "regular" beer. What was the name of this "contest?"

3. What company introduced the riveting frog commercials in 1995?

4. What soft drink did Britney Spears hawk in 2002?

5. Do you know the supreme entertainer who performed at halftime of Super Bowl XXX with a finale featuring her being taken from the stadium in a helicopter?

6. Can you name the mother-daughter country western team that highlighted the halftime show of Super Bowl XXVIII?

7. In 1993, Michael Jordan and Larry Bird went head to head playing a game of "Horse" in this commercial. What prize did the winner get?

8. In this 1997 spot, three pigeons see a shiny new auto pulling out of a carwash and attempt to "bomb" it. What kind of car was this?

9. Super Bowl XXV's halftime extravaganza featured what group in "A Small World Salute to 25 Years of the Super Bowl?"

10. What company boasted at the end of its 2000 Super Bowl commercial, "We just wasted two million dollars. What are you doing with your money?"

ANSWERS

1. Apple Computer (the commercial was for the Macintosh).

2. The Bud Bowl.

3. "Bud," "Weisssss," "Errrr."

4. Pepsi.

5. Diana Ross.

6. Wynonna & Naomi Judd.

7. A Big Mac.

8. A Nissan Maxima.

9. New Kids on the Block.

10. E*trade.

EXTRA POINT

"I feel like some guy who picked up a Rubik's Cube
and got it right the first time."

- ***Cris Collinsworth***, on being in the Super Bowl as a rookie

GIRL TALK

1. What Super Bowl XX quarterback's mother said to a reporter, "If you can figure him out, don't ask me. He has been a mystery since day one?"

2. Which former Texas governor did a Super Bowl XXIX Doritos commercial?

3. Who tossed the Super Bowl XV coin? Hint: she's the wife of a two-time Super Bowl-winning coach.

4. Who did an inebriated John Riggins tell to "lighten up" at a Washington, D.C. dinner?

5. What skater did Terry Bradshaw marry (and eventually divorce)?

6. Famous as an orange juice spokesperson in the late sixties, she became the first female to sing the national anthem at a Super Bowl (III). Do you know her?

7. Who's the 1971 Miss America that was an in-studio host for CBS-TV Super Bowl broadcasts?

8. Sandra Sexton's fifteen minute claim to fame came during halftime of Super Bowl IX. Do you remember it?

9. Who inspired Kansas City Chiefs owner Lamar Hunt to come up with the term Super Bowl?

10. Who's the only female owner to have a Super Bowl championship team?

ANSWERS

1. Jim McMahon's mother, Roberta.

2. Ann Richards.

3. Marie Lombardi.

4. Supreme Court Justice Sandra Day O'Connor.

5. Jo Jo Starbuck.

6. Anita Bryant.

7. Phyllis George.

8. She ran across the field in her bra and undies.

9. His daughter ... She was bouncing a rubber ball when Hunt asked what it was. She said, "That's a super ball, Daddy." Hunt then thought of "Super Bowl" and the rest is history.

10. Georgia Frontiere (the Rams).

EXTRA POINT

"We have a strange and wonderful relationship: he's strange and I'm wonderful."

*-**Mike Ditka**,* XX coach, about his relationship with quarterback Jim McMahon

DEE-FENSE!

1. What Colts Superbowl lineman starred in the *Police Academy* comedy films?

2. Do you know the Bills player who was credited with a safety against the Giants in XXV?

3. What two defensive players from the Cowboys shared the Super Bowl MVP award in 1978?

4. Who was the first player on a losing team to be named Super Bowl MVP?

5. Who were the front four of Pittsburgh's Super Bowl IX Steel Curtain defense?

6. What Cowboys defensive tackle was caught from behind as he attempted to showboat his way into the end zone after recovering a Bills fumble in Super Bowl XXVII?

7. In Super Bowl IX, what Viking blocked Steelers punter Bobby Walden's kick to result in Minnesota's only touchdown in the game?

8. In that same game, who led at the half, 2-0?

9. What quarterback has been intercepted the most in his Super Bowl career?

10. Name the Colts quarterback the Jets intercepted three times in the first half of Super Bowl III.

ANSWERS

1. Bubba Smith.

2. Bruce Smith.

3. Randy White and Harvey Martin.

4. Linebacker Chuck Howley of the Cowboys.

5. Mean Joe Greene, Ernie Holmes, L.C. Greenwood and Dwight White.

6. Leon Lett.

7. Matt Blair … Terry Brown picked up the blocked punt in the end zone for the TD.

8. The Steelers as they sacked Fran Tarkenton in the end zone for the only score of the half.

9. John Elway, 8.

10. Earl Morrall.

EXTRA POINT

"If we didn't have a huddle, Jim would have no social life."

-***Phil Simms***, about Giants' teammate Jim Burt

FACT OR FIB?

1. The Super Bowl is the most watched single-day sporting event.

2. A quarterback has been named MVP in more than half of all the Super Bowls that have been played.

3. People eat more food on Super Bowl Sunday than any other day of the year.

4. No team that has ever lost to the Tampa Bay Bucs in the regular season has won the Super Bowl.

5. Super Bowl quarterback Kurt Warner was bagging groceries and stocking shelves for $5.50 an hour in 1995, after his NFL career was seemingly at an end.

6. The first Super Bowl was slated for New York's Yankee Stadium, but then Mayor John Lindsay nixed the idea, scoffing that it would be "nothing more than a toilet bowl."

7. The first Super Bowl was actually called the AFL-NFL World Championship Game.

8. The big game has been telecast on four different networks.

9. The Super Bowl is broadcast to more than 50% of the world's countries.

10. The Patriots have appeared in three Super Bowls, all in New Orleans.

ANSWERS

1. Fact.

2. Fact.

3. Fib ... People eat more food on Super Bowl Sunday than any other day of the year other than Thanksgiving.

4. Fact.

5. Fact.

6. Fib.

7. Fact.

8. Fact ... ABC, CBS, FOX, and NBC.

9. Fact ... And, in fact, it's broadcast to 88% of the world's countries, 182.

10. Fact.

EXTRA POINT

"He carries so many tacklers with him, he's listed in the Yellow Pages under Public Transportation."

-*Bob Hope*, about Super Bowl XVIII MVP, running back *Marcus Allen*

INITIALLY SPEAKING

Identify these Super Bowl MVPs by their initials.

1. R.S. (VI)

2. L.S. (X)

3. D.W. (XXII)

4. J.R. (XXIII)

5. O.A. (XXV)

6. T.A. (XXVII)

7. E.S. (XXVIII)

8. S.Y. (XXIX)

9. T.D. (XXXII)

10. J.E. (XXXIII)

EXTRA POINT

"With so many Super Bowl rings,
maybe they'll all retire and go into the jewelry business."

-*John McKay*, about the Steelers

ANSWERS

1. Roger Staubach.

2. Lynn Swann.

3. Doug Williams.

4. Jerry Rice.

5. Ottis Anderson.

6. Troy Aikman.

7. Emmitt Smith.

8. Steve Young.

9. Terrell Davis.

10. John Elway.

EXTRA POINT

"More than being concerned with who's going to win the
Super Bowl, I feel the Lord is probably more concerned that
they might find a day other than Sunday to play it on."

-Billy Graham

T-FORMATION

The answers to these clues all have last names
which begin with the letter "T."

1. A broken leg busted up this Super Bowl quarterback's career.

2. "The Assassin" was a defensive back for the 1977 Super Bowl-winning Raiders.

3. This center played on all of Minnesota's Super Bowl teams in the '70s.

4. He played in three Super Bowls and is second only to Dan Marino in terms of regular season career passing yardage.

5. He scored the Chiefs final touchdown on a 46 yard pass from Len Dawson to seal a 23-7 victory over the Vikings in Super Bowl IV.

6. The most feared linebacker of his time, he played on the Giants when they were winners of Super Bowls XXI and XXV.

7. He was a defensive stalwart for the Buffalo Bills in all four of their Super Bowls in the '90s.

8. Another Buffalo player appeared in all of their Super Bowls in the '90s. He was the NFL's leading rusher in average yards per carry, 4.9, in 1991.

9. He kicked three field goals for the Jets in their huge upset of the Colts in Super Bowl III.

10. This Miami Dolphins wide receiver scored their first touchdown against Washington enroute to a 14-7 victory and an undefeated season.

ANSWERS

1. Joe Theismann.

2. Jack Tatum.

3. Mick Tingelhoff.

4. Fran Tarkenton.

5. Otis Taylor.

6. Lawrence Taylor.

7. Darryl Talley.

8. Thurman Thomas.

9. Jim Turner.

10. Howard Twilley.

EXTRA POINT

"I'm going to be in every weight-loss program available after football. I'll be into liposuction and ab-crunchers, and, if that doesn't work, then I'm going to stay in bed, eating, and have them bury me in a piano."

-*Nate Newton*, offensive lineman on the Cowboys Super Bowl teams of the '90s

THE NINETIES

1. Who passed for a record six touchdowns in Super Bowl XXIX in 1995?

2. What teams did the Bills lose to in the nineties?

3. Name the team which closed out the decade with back-to-back Super Bowl wins.

4. What team changed its name after the 1998 season and later appeared in a Super Bowl?

5. *The Sporting News* named what man, for whom a Super Bowl award is named, as the most powerful person in sports in the the 20th Century?

6. Who was the last player to catch a touchdown pass from John Elway?

7. Do you know the receiver Brett Favre connected with on a Super Bowl-record 81-yard touchdown for the Packers against the Patriots in 1997?

8. Can you name the man who became only the third head coach to win at least three Super Bowls when the Redskins became champs in 1992?

9. The Bills went on to the Super Bowl following their 1990 AFC title win, clobbering what team, 51-3?

10. What do Cher, Jewel, Luther Vandross and Vanessa Williams have in common?

ANSWERS

1. Steve Young.

2. The Giants, Redskins and Cowboys (twice).

3. Denver.

4. Tennessee changed its name from the Oilers to the Titans after which the NFL announced that the name Oilers would be retired - a first in league history.

5. Pete Rozelle.

6. Rod Smith, who caught an 80-yard TD pass in XXXIII.

7. Antonio Freeman.

8. Joe Gibbs.

9. The Raiders.

10. They all sang the national anthem at the Super Bowl.

EXTRA POINT

"He's the best thing to happen to Pittsburgh since U.S. Steel."

-*Jim Murray*, on Steeler Superbowler *Kordell Stewart*

MATCHMAKER, MATCHMAKER

*Listed below are NFL overall number one draft picks
who were also on the roster of Super Bowl teams.
Match the player with the college attended.*

1. Paul Hornung
2. Buck Buchanan
3. Bubba Smith
4. Ron Yary
5. John Matuszak
6. Ed "Too Tall" Jones
7. Kenneth Sims
8. Irving Fryar
9. Bruce Smith
10. Drew Bledsoe

a) USC
b) Houston
c) Notre Dame
d) Washington St.
e) Virginia Tech
f) Nebraska
g) Grambling
h) Michigan St.
i) Tennessee St.
j) Texas

EXTRA POINT

"It's ridiculous to get all worked up about a game -
except the Super Bowl, of course. Now that's important."

-Andy Rooney

ANSWERS

1. C (was on roster of Packers in Super Bowl I but did not play because of a pinched nerve).

2. G (Super Bowl IV with Chiefs).

3. H (III and V with Colts).

4. A (IV, VIII, IX and XI with Vikings).

5. B (XI and XV with Raiders).

6. I (X and XII with Cowboys).

7. J (XX with Patriots).

8. F (XX with Patriots).

9. E (XXV, XXVI, XXVII and XXVIII with Bills).

10. D (XXXI and XXXVI with Patriots).

EXTRA POINT

"What's the difference between a three-week-old puppy and a sportswriter? In six weeks, the puppy stops whining."

-Mike Ditka

NAME, PLEASE?

1. What's the real first name of the Bengals Super Bowl XXIII quarterback Boomer Esiason?

2. If the Pete Rozelle Trophy (for Super Bowl MVP) were engraved with the former commissioner's actual first name, what would it be called?

3. Who were nicknamed Butch Cassidy and the Sundance Kid?

4. What is Super Bowl-winning coach Weeb Ewbank's first name?

5. Who was known as "The Diesel"?

6. Although he spent most of his career with the Chargers, this player caught a touchdown pass for the Cowboys in their 24-3 Super Bowl win over Miami. His nickname is "Bambi". What's his real name?

7. Who is "Joe Willie"?

8. The "Wizard of Odds," Demetrios Synodinos is better known by what moniker?

9. Bobby Moore was a wide receiver on the Vikings Super Bowl XI team. How do you know him today?

10. Robert caught a 7-yard TD pass in Super Bowl XIII and recovered an onside kick with 17 seconds left to seal a 35-31 Pittsburgh win over Dallas. Can you identify him?

ANSWERS

1. Norman.

2. The Alvin Rozelle Trophy.

3. Miami's running backs, Jim Kiick (Butch) and Larry Csonka (Sundance Kid).

4. Wilbur.

5. John Riggins.

6. Lance Alworth.

7. Joe Namath.

8. That's the real name of the former Super Bowl handicapper, Jimmy the Greek.

9. As sportscaster Ahmad Rashad.

10. Rocky Bleier.

EXTRA POINT

"I'd run over Grimm's mother, too."

-*Matt Millen*, Raiders linebacker, after hearing that
Redskins offensive lineman *Russ Grimm* said
he'd run over his own mother to win Super Bowl XVII

BROACHING COACHING

*Where's Vanna when you need her? Replace the missing vowels in the
first and last names of the Super Bowl-winning coaches below.*

1. BLLBLCHCK

2. MKSHNHN

3. MKHLMGRN

4. GRGSFRT

5. CHCKNLL

6. DNSHL

7. JGBBS

8. BLLPRCLLS

9. MKDTK

10. DNMCCFFRTY

EXTRA POINT

"I feel like a rat in the cheese factory with the cat on vacation."

-Dallas' ***Thomas*** "Hollywood" ***Henderson***,
on playing in the Super Bowl

ANSWERS

1. Bill Belichick.

2. Mike Shanahan.

3. Mike Holmgren.

4. George Seifert.

5. Chuck Noll.

6. Don Shula.

7. Joe Gibbs.

8. Bill Parcells.

9. Mike Ditka.

10. Don McCafferty.

EXTRA POINT

"When you get old, everything is hurting. When I get up in the morning, it sounds like I'm making popcorn."

-Lawrence Taylor

LAUGH-IN TIME-OUT

It's time for one more trivia breather with these pigskin punch lines.

After Dallas Cowboys owner Jerry Jones dies and goes to heaven, God is taking him on a tour of the place. He shows Jerry a small three bedroom home with a tiny Cowboys pennant hanging over the front porch.

"This is your eternal home, Jerry," says God. "You should feel mighty proud because most folks don't get their own private living quarters here."

Jerry looks at the home, then does an about face and sees this huge four-story mansion with two gigantic Oakland Raiders Super Bowl Championship banners flying between four marble pillars. And parked in the circular driveway is a black and silver limo with the Raiders logo on the hood.

"Thanks for my home, God," says Jerry, "but I have just one question. You give me this tiny home with a miniature Cowboys pennant and my fellow owner Al Davis gets that beautiful mansion. How come?"

God laughs and says, "Oh, that's not Al Davis' home. That's mine."

"A friend gave me seats to the Super Bowl. From where I sat, the game was just a rumor." -Henny Youngman

LAUGH-IN TIME-OUT
(CONTINUED)

Q: Did you hear about the out-of-control Baltimore offensive lineman in Super Bowl XXXV?

A: He was a Raven lunatic.

A guy from San Francisco, a guy from Detroit and a guy from New Orleans are granted a talk with God. They're each allowed one question. The guy from San Francisco inquires, "Will there ever be a time when we don't have to worry about earthquakes?"

God responds, "Yes, but not in your lifetime."

Then the fellow from Detroit asks, "God, will there ever be a time when our city has no crime?"

Again God replies, "Yes, but not in your lifetime."

Finally, the guy from New Orleans asks, "God, will the Saints ever get to the Super Bowl?"

God answers, "Yes, but not in my lifetime!"

EXTRA POINT

"I feel so good about winning I'm almost weak."

-"Mean" *Joe Greene*, after the Steelers IX win

PIGSKIN POTPOURRI

1. Do you know the Super Bowl team named for a historical figure?

2. Who's the oldest coach to win a Super Bowl?

3. What Super Bowler was named *Sports Illustrated*'s Sportsman of the Year in 1990?

4. Until 1917, this Super Bowl venue was called the Pasadena Bowl. Name it.

5. What defensive lineman who played for the Cowboys in Super Bowl XII had a brief stint as a professional boxer, undefeated in six bouts?

6. Do you know the trumpeter who performed the National Anthem before Super Bowl IV in 1970?

7. What team has scored the most points in Super Bowl history?

8. Who was the first head coach to both win and lose a Super Bowl game?

9. What Super Bowl coach played NBA basketball?

10. Who's the only man to play on a national championship college team, coach a team to the national collegiate championship and be an NFL Super Bowl champion coach?

ANSWERS

1. The Buffalo Bills, for "Buffalo" Bill Cody.

2. Dick Vermeil, 63, when the Rams beat the Titans in XXXIV.

3. Joe Montana.

4. The Rose Bowl.

5. Ed "Too Tall" Jones.

6. Al Hirt.

7. The Dallas Cowboys, 221.

8. Hank Stram.

9. Bud Grant ... He delayed an NFL career to play for the Minneapolis Lakers basketball team for the 1950-51 season.

10. Jimmy Johnson, who played for Arkansas in 1964, coached the Miami Hurricanes to a national title in 1987, and guided the Dallas Cowboys to two Super Bowl wins.

EXTRA POINT

"I was thinking I had just crossed the goal line."

-*Roger Craig*, when asked what his thoughts were after scoring a touchdown in Super Bowl XIX

MULTIPLE CHOICE

1. He tossed 122 passes in four Super Bowls without ever throwing an interception. a) Joe Montana b) Steve Young c) Bart Starr d) Ringo Starr

2. Which Super Bowl coach was one of the "Seven Blocks of Granite" at Fordham? a) Weeb Ewbank b) Vince Lombardi c) Bud Grant d) Hugh Grant

3. He and his mom starred in Campbell's Chunky Soup commercials after his sterling performance in Super Bowl XXXII. a) John Elway b) Ed McCaffrey c) Terrell Davis d) Sammy Davis, Jr.

4. This quarterback led the Raiders to two Super Bowl victories in the '80s after being cut by the 49ers. a) Ken Stabler b) Jim Plunkett c) Steve Young d) Cy Young

5. A defensive lineman from Texas Christian, he played in Super Bowls V and VI and was the first draft pick in his team's history. a) Bob Lilly b) Gino Marchetti c) Deacon Jones d) Tom Jones

6. He was the coach of New England's Super Bowl XX team and was selected as a wide receiver on the NFL's 75th Anniversary All-Time Team. a) Don Hutson b) Jack Snow c) Raymond Berry d) Halle Berry

7. Elbert (his real first name) never did get to do his "shuffle" in Super Bowl XXIII. a) Bam Morris b) Ironhead Heyward c) Ickey Woods d) Tiger Woods

8. At 45 he was the oldest player to suit up for a Super Bowl. a) George Blanda b) Steve DeBerg c) Dave Jennings d) Peter Jennings

9. This Super Bowl quarterback began his professional career with the USFL's Houston Gamblers. a) Jim Kelly b) Steve Young c) Doug Williams d) Ted Williams

10. When this Super Bowl running back scored 25 touchdowns during the '95 season, he broke John Riggins' record of 24. a) Franco Harris b) Marcus Allen c) Emmitt Smith d) Jaclyn Smith

ANSWERS

1. A.

2. B.

3. C.

4. B.

5. A ... Lilly was picked by the Dallas Cowboys in 1961. Though the club began play in 1960, their first draft wasn't until the following year.

6. C.

7. C.

8. B.

9. A.

10. C.

EXTRA POINT

"You're only great if you win something. Alexander wasn't Alexander the Mediocre or Alexander the Average. He was Alexander the Great, and there's a reason for it."

-Sterling Sharpe, about the significance of winning the Super Bowl

SCREEN TEST

1. The broadcast crew for ABC's Super Bowl telecast in 1985 consisted of Frank Gifford, Don Meredith and which then-still-active quarterback?

2. Robert Urich portrayed what Vietnam vet, Super Bowl running back in the made-for-TV movie *Fighting Back*?

3. In that same movie, Art Carney played the owner of the running back's team. Name him.

4. Was Howard Cosell ever in the broadcast booth for a Super Bowl game?

5. The 1977 thriller *Black Sunday* incorporated actual footage from which Super Bowl?

6. Which two teams met in a fictional Super Bowl at the end of *Heaven Can Wait* before meeting for real in Super Bowl XIV?

7. What Super Bowl XIX quarterback and his team figured prominently in the 1994 comedy flick *Ace Ventura: Pet Detective*?

8. The opposing coaches of Super Bowl XXX had cameos in the goofball comedy *The Waterboy*. Can you name them?

9. Name the Super Bowl MVP quarterback who had roles in three Burt Reynolds movies: *Hooper*, *The Cannonball Run* and *Smokey and the Bandit II*.

10. Another Super Bowl MVP shared a motorcycle and a relationship with Ann-Margret in the 1970 film *CC and Company*. Who is he?

ANSWERS

1. Joe Theismann.

2. Rocky Bleier.

3. Art Rooney.

4. No.

5. Super Bowl X, with the Steeler and Cowboys.

6. The Steelers and Rams.

7. Dan Marino and the Dolphins.

8. Jimmy Johnson and Bill Cowher.

9. Terry Bradshaw.

10. Joe Namath.

EXTRA POINT

"Do we have to start at one?"

-Dallas coach *Tom Landry*, when asked to rate
the poor performance by the Cowboys' secondary
on a scale of one to ten

BY THE NUMBERS

Provide the answer based on the clue and the player's uniform number.

1. 88- Scored St. Louis' first ever Super Bowl touchdown.

2. 24- Intercepted a pass and returned it for the first TD of Super Bowl XXXVI.

3. 66- Played on the champion Packer teams of I and II.

4. 27- Scored two TDs for the Titans in XXXIV.

5. 13- Set a single game record for throwing the most passes, 45, without an interception.

6. 55- Chargers linebacker in XXIX.

7. 32- Raiders running back who rushed for 191 yards on 20 carries in XVIII.

8. 87- Played on two 49ers Super Bowl teams.

9. 13- A Super Bowl III participant, his number's been retired by the Jets.

10. 83- Had a 94-yard TD kickoff return for Falcons in XXXIII.

<hr />

EXTRA POINT

"In one of the greatest games in history - by one team ..."

-Broadcaster **Brent Musburger**, after the 49ers manhandled the Broncos in Super Bowl XXIV

ANSWERS

1. Torry Holt.

2. Ty Law.

3. Ray Nitschke.

4. Eddie George.

5. Kurt Warner.

6. Junior Seau.

7. Marcus Allen.

8. Dwight Clark.

9. Don Maynard.

10. Tim Dwight.

EXTRA POINT

"We consider our Super Bowl trophy an antique."

-Steelers coach **Chuck Noll**, on the season opener
after winning the previous year's big game

HI HO, SILVER!

Here's a quiz about The Super Bowl Silver Anniversary Team which was chosen by the fans in 1990 prior to XXV.

1. This man was chosen as head coach for this elite team. He won two Super Bowls and finished up his career with the Washington Redskins but you know him better from another team. Who is he?

2. One of the running backs selected played on four Super Bowl winners. Can you name him?

3. The anniversary team's tight end is nicknamed "The Ghost" and had an 11-year career, mostly with the Raiders. Do you know him?

4. One of the team's offensive tackles played on and later coached the Raiders. Who is he?

5. The two defensive ends who made the team played against each other in Super Bowl X when the Steelers defeated the Cowboys, 21-17. One was drafted in the tenth round in 1969 by the Steelers, the other a first round pick of Dallas in 1974. Do you know either one?

6. This one should be a gimme - The quarterback selected wound up his career with the Chiefs, and in addition to this selection, is a member of the NFL's 75th Anniversary All-Time Team. Name him.

7. One of the guards named to the team was a member of the Packers and authored the book *Instant Replay*. Who is he?

8. What 13-year Steeler veteran (1970-83) was selected for one of the cornerback positions?

9. A pair of Jacks were chosen for one of the inside and one of the outside linebacker positions. Can you name these two Steelers?

10. Only one member of the Bears made the team, an inside linebacker in Super Bowl XX. Do you know him?

ANSWERS

1. Vince Lombardi.

2. Franco Harris.

3. Dave Casper.

4. Art Shell.

5. L.C. Greenwood and Too Tall Jones.

6. Joe Montana.

7. Jerry Kramer.

8. Mel Blount.

9. Jack Lambert (inside linebacker) and Jack Ham (outside linebacker).

10. Mike Singletary.

EXTRA POINT

"I was watching the Super Bowl with my 92-year old grandfather. The team scored a touchdown.
They showed the instant replay. He thought they scored another one. I was gonna tell him, but I figured the game he was watching was better."

-Steven Wright

Y2K AND BEYOND

1. What was the final score of the Rams victory over Tennessee in 2000?

2. Who tackled Kevin Dyson at the 1-yard line as time expired to preserve St. Louis' win in that game?

3. The winning coaches of the 2001 and 2002 Super Bowls have the same initials. What are their names?

4. In 2006, the Super Bowl will be held in Detroit at what facility?

5. Where was the 2001 Super Bowl between the Ravens and Giants played?

6. Can you name the Raven who intercepted a Kerry Collins pass and returned it 49 yards for a touchdown?

7. What "Fab Four" performer led a Super Bowl XXXVI pre-game performance to honor the the game's celebration of the heroism following the events of September 11th, 2001?

8. How did the National Car Dealers Association figure in the delay of Super Bowl XXXVI?

9. Fill in the blank: When the Patriots-Rams game was played in New Orleans, it marked the ___ time that the Super Bowl had been played in the Crescent City.

10. Who's the owner of the Super Bowl XXXVI champion Patriots?

ANSWERS

1. 23-16.

2. Mike Jones.

3. Brian Billick and Bill Belichick.

4. Ford Field.

5. Raymond James Stadium.

6. Duane Starks.

7. Paul McCartney.

8. The game, slated for the Superdome in New Orleans, was postponed a week because of the September 11th terrorist attacks. The NFL paid the National Car Dealers Association $7.5 million to move its convention to accommodate the change.

9. 9th.

10. Robert Kraft.

EXTRA POINT

"Don Shula can take his'n and beat you'n, and he could take you'n and beat his'n."

-Bum Phillips

PIGSKIN POTPOURRI

1. What distinction do Chuck Howley of the Cowboys and Bobby Richardson of baseball's Yankees share regarding championship teams?

2. The Chicago Bears, Super Bowl XX champs, went 15-1 in 1985, losing only to whom?

3. What NFL head coach won three Super Bowls before retiring from football to become the owner of a NASCAR racing team?

4. What 16-year veteran, playing for the Cowboys, dropped a sure touchdown pass in the Super Bowl against the Steelers as Pittsburgh beat Dallas, 35-31?

5. He holds the record for the longest run from scrimmage in a regular season game, 99 yards, and played for Dallas in Super Bowls XII and XIII. Name him.

6. What did the town of Ismay, Montana, become in 1993?

7. What Super Bowl record does defensive lineman Mike Lodish hold?

8. Who's the only quarterback to play in five Super Bowls?

9. Super Bowl XXVII (1993) was originally slated to be played in Phoenix, but was changed to Pasadena. Why?

10. Three teams from the NFL became part of the American Football Conference when the NFL and AFL merged. One of them has yet to play in a Super Bowl. Can you name that team?

ANSWERS

1. They were both MVPs for a losing cause - Howley in Super Bowl V and Richardson for the 1960 Yankees.

2. The Dolphins.

3. Joe Gibbs.

4. Jackie Smith.

5. Tony Dorsett.

6. The town changed its name to Joe, Montana, in honor of the three-time Super Bowl MVP.

7. He's had the most Super Bowl appearances, six (four with the Bills, two with the Broncos).

8. John Elway.

9. Because the state of Arizona had vetoed a holiday for Martin Luther King, Jr's birthday.

10. The Browns … The other teams were the Pittsburgh Steelers and the Colts (then of Baltimore).

EXTRA POINT

"If every game was a Super Bowl,
Joe Montana would be undefeated."

-Randy Cross

ALL IN THE FAMILY

1. Name the only father and son to coach against each other in an NFL game. Hint: the father coached more than one Super Bowl team.

2. What brother combination, both of whom have played in Super Bowls, holds the distinction of scoring the most points in pro football history?

3. He was a one year quarteback with the Houston Oilers in 1980 while his brother won four Super Bowl rings as a QB from 1970-1983. Can you identify their last name?

4. This Hall of Fame running back gained 62 yards in XX and his brother was a running back and kick returner in the NFL for four teams over a five year period. What are their names?

5. This pair of brothers played on the same team, the Bengals. One was a two-time Heisman trophy-winning running back who played in a Super Bowl while his brother was a defensive back. Name them.

6. Who was in the broadcast booth while his wife sang the national anthem at Super Bowl XXIX?

7. One brother was a wide receiver, the other a tight end who played in Super Bowl XXXII. Can you name this pair of all-pros?

8. He was a running back on the Eagles in XV. His brother Cleo was a kick returner with the Raiders in XVIII. Another brother, Tyrone, was a reserve running back with the Raiders for two years. Who is that Eagle?

9. True or false? Quarterback Steve Young, XXIX's MVP, is the great-great-great grandson of Brigham Young.

10. This center played in Super Bowls with the Giants and 49ers and his brother had a six-year career in the NFL, also as an offensive linemen. Who are they?

ANSWERS

1. Don and David Shula.

2. Matt and Chris Bahr.

3. Bradshaw ... Terry and Craig.

4. Walter and Eddie Payton.

5. Archie and Ray Griffin ... A third brother, Keith, was a running back for the Redskins and Falcons.

6. Frank Gifford ... Kathie Lee performed the national anthem.

7. Sterling and Shannon Sharpe.

8. Wilbert Montgomery.

9. True.

10. Bart and Brad Oates.

EXTRA POINT

"If a nuclear bomb is dropped on this country,
the only thing I'm sure will survive
will be Astroturf and Don Shula."

-*Bubba Smith*, on the Super Bowl coach

TOUCHDOWN TOMES

*Match each of the Super Bowlers, from player
to coach to ref, with the book he authored.
(In some cases, the word "authored" is used very loosely.)*

1. Jack Tatum

2. Bill Parcells

3. Vince Lombardi

4. Joe Namath

5. Joe Theismann

6. Reggie White

7. Doug Williams

8. Roger Staubach

9. Don Shula

10. Paul Hornung

a) *In the Trenches*

b) *Quarterback: Shattering the NFL Myth*

c) (name here): *Time Enough to Win*

d) *Quarterbacking*

e) *They Call Me Assassin*

f) *Football and the Single Man*

g) *The Winning Edge*

h) *I Can't Wait Until Tomorrow 'Cause I Get Better Looking Every Day*

i) *Run to Daylight*

j) (last name here): *Autobiography of the Biggest Giant of Them All*

EXTRA POINT

"He has two speeds - here he comes and there he goes."

-*Barry Wilborn*, about *Roy Green*

ANSWERS

1. E.

2. J.

3. I.

4. H.

5. D.

6. A.

7. B.

8. C.

9. G.

10. F. (As mentioned earlier, Hornung was on the Packers roster but didn't play in Super Bowl I.)

EXTRA POINT

"After that game, we could have played the Girl Scouts and we wouldn't have taken it as a joke."

-John Mackey, after the 17 1/2 point favorite Colts lost to the Jets in III

LOCATION, LOCATION, LOCATION!

Listed below are Super Bowls, dates, teams and scores.
Your task is to name the stadium in which the game was played.

Super Bowl	Date	Teams and Score
1. V	1-17-71	Baltimore 16, Dallas 13
2. VII	1-14-73	Miami 14, Washington 7
3. XI	1-9-77	Oakland 32, Minnesota 14
4. XIII	1-21-79	Pittsburgh 35, Dallas 31
5. XV	1-25-81	Oakland 27, Philadelphia 10
6. XIX	1-20-85	San Francisco 38, Miami 16
7. XXII	1-31-88	Washington 42, Denver 10
8. XXIX	1-29-95	San Francisco 49, San Diego 26
9. XXX	1-28-96	Dallas 27, Pittsburgh 17
10. XXXIV	1-30-00	St. Louis 23, Tennessee 16

EXTRA POINT

"It has been my experience that the fastest man on the
football field is the quarterback who has just
had his pass intercepted."

-Barry Switzer

ANSWERS

1. Orange Bowl, Miami.

2. Memorial Coliseum, Los Angeles.

3. Rose Bowl, Pasadena.

4. Orange Bowl, Miami.

5. Superdome, New Orleans.

6. Stanford Stadium, Stanford.

7. Jack Murphy Stadium (now Qualcomm Stadium), San Diego.

8. Joe Robbie Stadium (now Pro Player Stadium), Miami.

9. Sun Devil Stadium, Tempe.

10. Georgia Dome, Atlanta.

EXTRA POINT

"I don't think there are going to be that many people writing books this year. We don't have that many people who can read and write."

-Cornerback **Mark Collins**, about the difference between the New York Giants Super Bowl XXI and XXV championship teams

WHO YOU TALKIN' 'BOUT II?

Once again, see if you can figure out the subject of the quote.
As a hint, we've included the Super Bowl team with
which they're associated, be it as a player, owner, coach, etc.

1. "When _____ goes on safari, the lions roll up the windows." (Dolphins) -*Monte Clark*

2. "_____ is the kind of guy who would steal your eyes and then try to convince you that you looked better without them." (Raiders) -*Sam Rutigliano*

3. "Since we're a one-man team, _____ has a curfew. The rest can do what they want." (Broncos) -*Dan Reeves*

4. "About 310 pounds, eyes of blue, about the cutest thing you ever saw." (Bears) -*Mike Ditka*

5. "_____ was on *Wild Kingdom* once and they shot him." (Steelers) -*Don Rickles*

6. "_____ faked me out so bad one time that I got a 15-yard penalty for grabbing my own face mask." (Steelers) -*D.D. Lewis*

7. "_____ has more touchdowns than NASA." (49ers) -*Roy Firestone*

8. "Describing _____ as intense is like describing the universe as fairly large." (Colts/Dolphins)

9. "He's such a perfectionist that if he were married to Dolly Parton, he'd expect her to cook." (Cowboys) -*Don Meredith*

10. "You don't need a tape measure to register his hits, you need a seismograph." (49ers) -*Jim Murray*

ANSWERS

1. Larry Csonka.

2. Al Davis.

3. John Elway.

4. William "Refrigerator" Perry.

5. "Mean" Joe Greene.

6. Franco Harris.

7. Jerry Rice.

8. Don Shula.

9. Tom Landry.

10. Ronnie Lott.

EXTRA POINT

"That's one way to look at it.
The other is that I haven't had a promotion in 21 years."

- *Tom Landry*, on coaching the Dallas Cowboys for 21 years
(five times in the Super Bowl)

MINDING YOUR P'S AND Q'S

*The list below contains p's and q's which have already been noted.
Using the clues given, fill in the blanks.*

1. __ __ __ __   __ P __ __ __ __
   Lone Raider to appear in Super Bowls II, XI, and XV.

2. __ __ __ __   __ __ P __ __
   He was born Mark Kirby Dupas and played in XIX.

3. __ __ __ __   __ __ Q __ __
   Frenchy, the running back who was on Steelers of IX and X.

4. P __ __   P __ __ __ __ __
   Falcons made their lone Super Bowl appearance, a loss, in
   this stadium.

5. __ __ __ __   __ __ P __ __ __ __ __
   Scored all of Miami's points against Cowboys in VI.

6. __ __ __ __   __ Q__ __ __ __ __
   Intercepted a Joe Theismann pass and returned it for a TD
   in XVIII.

7. __ __ __   P __ __ __ __ __ __ __
   Quarterbacked Raiders to victory in XV.

8. Q __ __ __ __ __ __ __   __ __ __ __ __ __ __
   Broncos won their first Super Bowl here.

9. __ __ __ __ __ __   __ __ __ P__ __
   Caught Pittsburgh's lone touchdown pass in XXX.

10. __ __ __ __   __ __ P __ __ __
    MVP of XXVI when Skins beat the Bills.

ANSWERS

1. Gene Upshaw.

2. Mark "Super" Duper.

3. John Fuqua.

4. Pro Player.

5. Garo Yepremian.

6. Jack Squirek.

7. Jim Plunkett.

8. Qualcomm Stadium.

9. Yancey Thigpen.

10. Mark Rypien.

EXTRA POINT

"I don't say my folks were poor, but when my uncle used to slice ham at dinner, it had only one side."

- ***Walt Garrison***, running back on the
Super Bowl V and VI Cowboys

LAST CALL

You probably recall the Super Bowl teams of the players listed below, but can you identify the last team they played for in their careers?

1. Ronnie Lott

2. James Lofton

3. John Mackey

4. Franco Harris

5. Art Monk

6. Jim Ringo

7. Johnny Unitas

8. Jim Taylor

9. Herb Adderley

10. Forrest Gregg

EXTRA POINT

"I guess the first time I three-putt."

-***Mike Ditka***, on when he'd begin to think about the following season after winning the Super Bowl

ANSWERS

1. Jets, 1994.

2. Eagles, 1993.

3. Chargers, 1972.

4. Seahawks, 1984.

5. Eagles, 1995.

6. Eagles, 1967.

7. Chargers, 1973.

8. Saints, 1967.

9. Cowboys, 1972.

10. Cowboys, 1971.

EXTRA POINT

"You've got to like any job
where you don't have to go to work until noon."

-Super Bowl MVP *John Riggins*

BOWL GAMES

*Appropriately enough, this is a bonus quiz of
bathroom-related questions. Here goes...*

1. Before the 1986 Super Bowl, what network gave viewers a blank screen to enable them to go to the bathroom?

2. "The U.S. Congress can declare war with a simple majority, but we need a three-quarters majority to go to the john." Griping about what it takes to revise NFL rules, this was said by the owner of the Ravens, Super Bowl XXXV champs. Name him.

3. When Denver won the 1977 AFC title, the city's fans developed an "Orange Crush" on their team, many of whom sent orange-colored toilet seats to the Broncos head coach, whose name is of a different color. Do you know him?

4. What Super Bowl teams have played home games in Flushing?

5. His name may not be quite as famous as the toilet paper maker (hint, hint), but he was definitely on a roll in the 1973 Super Bowl when he was selected MVP of the game. Can you name this defensive back?

6. "Supposedly, he weighs 325. Hey, who knows? He's running twice a day - from the refrigerator to the bathroom." Bears coach Mike Ditka said this about the off-season conditioning of what Super Bowl player?

7. True or false? New York City water pressure dropped due to toilet flushing after the Giants-Broncos Super Bowl game.

8. Within 20, can you guess how many bathrooms are in the New Orleans Superdome?

9. Where did Carroll Rosenbloom give Pete Rozelle the news that he'd been elected NFL commissioner?

10. Is it true that Joe Namath was signed to a pro contract in a hotel bathroom?

ANSWERS

1. NBC.

2. Art Modell.

3. Red Miller.

4. The Jets and Giants ... Shea Stadium is in Flushing, a section of Queens which is one of the five boroughs of New York City.

5. Jake Scott, who intercepted two passes for Miami in their win over Washington.

6. William "Refrigerator" Perry.

7. False ... Just before the game, Harvey Schultz, commissioner of the NYC Department of Environmental Protection, issued a "bowl warning." Schultz suggested that Super Bowl viewers should can, or at least curb, their trips to the john so the city's water system wouldn't be under too much pressure. A Big Apple p.r. person admitted later that the warning was nothing more than a media prank.

8. 104 (52 men's and 52 women's rooms).

9. You guessed it - in the bathroom. Rosenbloom, then the owner of the Baltimore Colts, told Rozelle in the men's room of a Miami beach hotel on January 26, 1960. (Rozelle was washing his hands at the time.)

10. Yes ... As the story goes, Namath, Sonny Werblin (then the president of the Jets), and attorneys were present in a hotel room. While the lawyers were bickering over details, Namath headed for the bathroom and motioned for Werblin to follow him. Behind closed door, Namath asked Werblin if he had another copy of the contract. Werblin did and Namath signed it.